Being
Mummy

Wakefield Press
1 The Parade West
Kent Town
South Australia 5067
www.wakefieldpress.com.au

First published 2007

Scans by Graphic Print Group, Adelaide
Designed by Liz Nicholson, designBITE
Illustrations by Emily Bollen
Printed in China at Everbest Printing Co Ltd

ISBN 978 1 86254 747 6

Photo credits: Front cover – Kate Elmes, Back cover – Mick Bradley,
Inside jacket flap – Kate Elmes, Author photograph – Roger Taplin.
Kate Elmes' photographs feature on pages 5, 6, 9, 13, 14, 18, 21, 22, 25, 30, 37, 38, 41,
50, 53, 54, 55, 62, 66, 69, 70, 73, 77, 81, 82, 86, 93, 94, 98. flnriver@llnet.com.au
Mick Bradley's photographs feature on pages 10, 17, 26, 29, 33, 45, 46,
57, 58, 61, 65, 78, 85, 89, 90, 97. www.mickbradley.com
Roger Taplin's photographs feature on pages 34, 74, 100.
Anne-marie Taplin's photographs feature on pages 42 and 49.

Government of South Australia
Arts SA

fox creek

Being Mummy

Anne-marie Taplin

Photographs by Kate Elmes and Mick Bradley

Wakefield
Press

I love more intensely
than I thought possible.

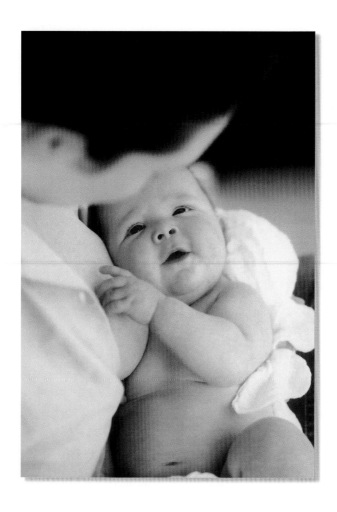

Seeing my child's face
first thing in the morning
is the light of my day.

I spend hours gazing
at my baby.

I know that everything changes,
and it's usually too quickly.

I've realised a dog
is no substitute for a child
(or even a practice run).

Every day and every week
has a rhythm and its own pace
and it has nothing to do
with the world outside.

I've learned to read aloud.

I've realised the English
language can be silly.

I've learned to sing.

I feel the weight of responsibility.

Multi-tasking is the name
of the game.

Silence is golden.

I realise now that child rearing
is the hardest work there is,
and also the least recognised.

Sometimes I can't cope and I
just want to escape . . .
if only for a day.

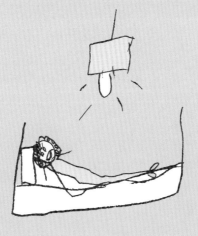

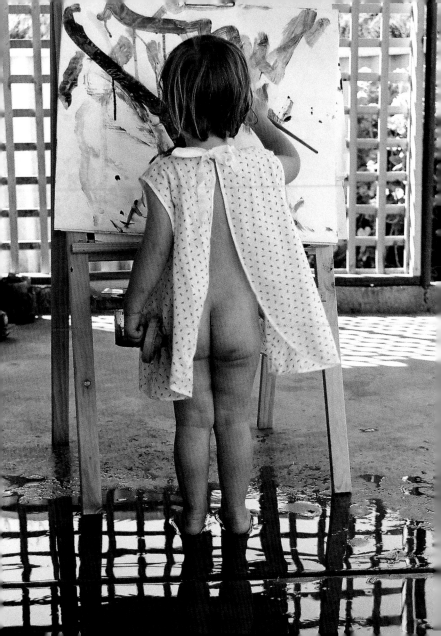

My life is separated into
BC and AC:
Before Children and After Children.

My home is child-friendly
and often messy.

There's no longer any such
luxury as personal space.

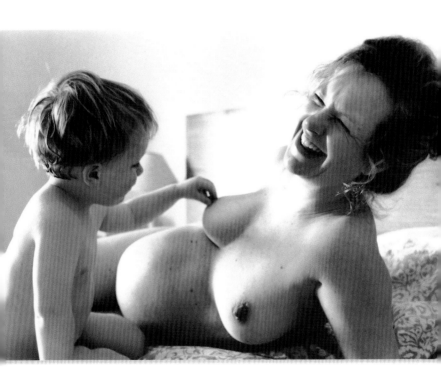

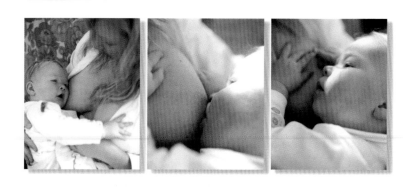

I've never known such
bittersweet unrequited love
for it's only natural that my
children won't always love me
as much as I love them.

I wonder how so many years
passed in the days before children.

I value every precious
moment with my children
(or at least I try to).

Capturing the present has never
seemed so important.

Life has new meaning.

I've discovered a small body in
the bed can be warm and snuggly
or cold and wriggly.

Being with other adults is no longer the norm for me.

It takes forever to leave the house.

I am caged and bound by children where once I was free in ways that I didn't appreciate.

My days are filled with constant
noise, demands, tears
and laughter.

I have less time for friends,
especially those without children.

I realise now that all those lyrics
to love songs are about what
a mother feels for her child.

I plan for the future with new
purpose, hope and fear.

I value the relationship
with my parents more.

I have things in better perspective.

Beauty is my child's face.

Keeping a record of every milestone
is now second nature.

I don't sleep as often or as well
and when I do, it's usually broken.

No kiss tastes as sweet
as my baby's.

Everything in the world has the
potential to influence my child,
so I've become very choosey.

Whole days can pass in our
pyjamas.

I can have lots of fun
being really silly.

'Tired' is my middle name.

Sometimes I feel consumed
from all directions.

I value my own life more . . .
I fear losing it and the
consequences for my children.

I place greater value on
where I live and consciously
choose to stay.

I can't talk on the phone any more, except when the children are in bed!

I'm fascinated by topics that previously I found irrelevant and boring.

I feel the neglect, abuse or
murder of any child in my gut . . .
the anguish is both personal
and universal.

I have learned to hold
two conversations at once.

The question 'Why?'
is part of my daily life
and often I have to think very
hard about how to answer it!

Sometimes I have less patience,
especially at the end of the week
when I've been responsible for
the children for 10 hours a day.

I think about what age I'll be
when my child is 10 or 20 years old.

The feel of my child's hand in mine
is wonderful.

My own and my partner's faults
and inadequacies are magnified
(at least in my mind).

I know now that the hard work
starts after the birth.

The funniest joke in the world
can come from the mouth
of a three-year-old.

I'm more careful.

I drive more safely.

I think more about my own
upbringing and the adult
I have become.

I yearn for solitude
but I miss my children madly
when we are apart.

I am not as selfish, in fact
my needs usually come last.

I see myself in another face.

I cry so easily!
There is a well of emotion inside
that often threatens to engulf me.

A good night's sleep is a rare
and precious thing.

Being at home can be
fun, insulating, relaxed,
boring or isolating . . .
depending on how
the day is going.

Good manners matter.

Birth stories fascinate me.

I don't stay up late any more.

I'm more afraid, because I have
so much more to lose.

Protecting our environment
and creating a better world
now has greater significance.

There is no 'safe zone' . . .
having a child means being
forever vulnerable to pain.

I realise that time can be
measured in how much
your child changes.

I want to sleep when I can't
and when I can, I don't want to.

A child crying is the most
distressing sound in the world
and impossible to ignore.

Catching up for coffee is a luxury
of the past.

I think about how my friends will
affect my children and how
my children will affect my friends.

My body has changed,
mostly for the worse.

I don't value my career as highly.

I have less time for my partner
and less energy for 'us'.

I think more about life,
education, values and
my role as a teacher of
the next generation.

I've realised that there
should be many more words
for 'love' and 'beauty'.

I've realised how much
I don't know.

I have permission to play
childish games.

I know that I am
incredibly lucky.

My patience, resolutions and beliefs are tested to the limits, sometimes daily.

Enjoying a nice dinner is impossible with the children around.

I feel fulfilled in a way that
I'd never dreamed possible.

Hugging my child
is just not close enough.

I value my personal time
in ways that I couldn't have
imagined before.

I take better care of my own
health because I want to be
around for as long as possible.

I laugh and sometimes cry
on a daily basis,
often many times a day!

'I' have something in common with
every other mother on the planet
– and we can talk about it.

Hearing my child say
'I love you'
makes every sacrifice
worthwhile.

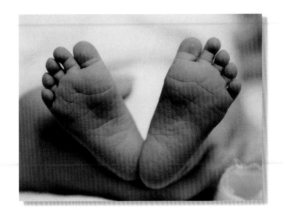

For Harry and Georgie
because everything worth knowing,
I have learned from them.